The Absolutely True, Positively Awesome Book About . . . ME!!!

By ME!!!

(with help from JESSICA WILBER)

Edited by Elizabeth Verdick & Jessica Thoreson

Library of Congress Cataloging-in-Publication Data
Wilber, Jessica, 1981–
The absolutely true, positively awesome book about—Me! / by Me (with help from Jessica Wilber)
p. cm.
Includes bibliographical references and index.
Summary: Presents ideas and advice on keeping a journal, along with related activities.
ISBN 1-57542-061-9
1. Diaries—Authorship—Juvenile literature. [1. Diaries.] I. Title.
PN4390.W54 1999
808′.06692—dc21 98-54593
CIP
AC

Cover and illustrations by Marieka Heinlen
Interior design by Jessica Thoreson
Index prepared by Diana Witt

10 9 8 7 6 5 4 3 2 1

Printed in the United States of America

Free Spirit Publishing Inc.
400 First Avenue North, Suite 616
Minneapolis, MN 55401-1724
(612) 338-2068
help4kids@freespirit.com
www.freespirit.com

Dedication

This book is dedicated to Grandma Daniel.

Acknowledgments

I would like to thank my mom and dad,
all the people at Free Spirit Publishing, and all my friends and family members for helping me when I needed it. I couldn't have done it without you.

I'd also like to thank all the girls
who read and were inspired by my first book.

Contents

Dear Reader,

I remember what it was like to be a girl your age. I was seven, eight, and nine not very long ago. It's fun to look back at what my life was like then. I do this by reading my past journal entries.

I've kept a journal for years. Because of my journal, I can remember many things I might have forgotten. I know myself better. I can see how I've changed over the years. And journaling has given me a book of memories, all about me.

I hope you enjoy creating an absolutely true, positively awesome book about YOU. Happy journaling!

Sincerely,

P.S. You can contact me at this address:

Jessica Wilber
c/o Free Spirit Publishing Inc.
400 First Avenue North, Suite 616
Minneapolis, MN 55401-1724

Or you can email me at: *help4kids@freespirit.com*

April 24
YOU WILL FIND GREAT HAPPINESS.
i think journaling is important because

Why Journaling Is Important

I think keeping a journal is a great thing to do. Why? Because my journal is a place where I can talk to myself. When I read past entries, I see how much I've changed. To me, that's pretty important. Journal writing matters for a lot of reasons. You may agree with my ideas, or you may have some of your own. Start a journal entry with "I think journaling is important because . . ." and see where your thoughts take you.

Journaling Can Help You . . .

Remember things. Because of my journal, I have memories of all sorts of things that I would have forgotten otherwise.

Understand yourself. In your journal, you'll probably write about things that are important to you. You may notice patterns of feelings, thoughts, and ideas. Looking at what you've written can help you get to know yourself better.

Handle your feelings. A journal is a good place to sort through all your feelings, like happiness, sadness, or anger. In your journal, you can write about what made you feel a certain way and why.

Like yourself. After you've been journaling for a while, look back at some of the things you've written or drawn. You might see that you're a very creative person with a lot of great ideas. This can make you feel good!

Journaling Tips

Date every entry. (This is really important.) You may think you'll always remember the date something happened, but it's surprising how quickly you can forget.

Write whenever you feel like it, whether that's twice a day or once a month. Don't feel like you have to write every day. When you want to write, do it!

A journal entry can be long or short. You may need pages and pages or only one sentence to talk about your feelings and ideas. Write as much or as little as you want.

Today i went to
Melissa's house-
it was fun.

★ Ideas for Your Journal ★

You don't have to keep your journal in a one-year diary with a lock and one tiny page for each day. You'll need a lot more space if you really want to be creative. This section will help you figure out what kind of journal is right for you.

"Book" Journals

I like a journal that's more like a book because there's plenty of room to be creative. You might want to try one of these "book" journals.

A blank book. There are many types of blank books, large and small. You can choose the one that suits you best. I like a journal without lines so I can write and draw. It can be fun to get a blank book covered with solid-colored cloth, then decorate the cover with fabric markers or glitter paint.

A three-ring binder. A three-ring binder is great because you can keep all sorts of things in it. You can use dividers with pockets to separate your binder into sections. You can also buy different kinds of pages to put in it.

A notebook. A small spiral notebook makes a good journal. One nice thing about this kind of journal is that you can take it with you and write in it almost anywhere. You can decorate the cover however you want. But if you get a notebook with lines, you might want to have a separate blank book or sketch pad for drawing. It's up to you.

"*Awed, unique,* and *proud* were three words that she had written on page seven of her green notebook. She kept lists of her favorite words; she kept important private information; and she kept things that she thought might be the beginnings of poems, in her green notebook."

from *Anastasia Krupnik* by Lois Lowry

A Computer Journal

A computer journal is a lot of fun. You can type in many different fonts and sizes, and even spice up your journal with computerized illustrations called clip art. If you don't have a computer at home, you might be able to use one at a local library. Be sure to save your computer journal on a disk, and keep the disk in a safe place. This is especially important if you don't want anyone else to read what you've written. Make two copies of the disk in case something happens to one of them.

If you are planning to keep a computer journal (or any other kind of journal that doesn't use paper), you might want to have a notebook and a sketch pad, too. That way, you can still journal when you're away from your computer.

A Journal on Tape

A cassette or videotape journal can be fun to try even if you don't want to keep one all the time. For a cassette tape journal, just leave a journal tape in your boombox. Plug in a microphone, and you're ready to go. Or you might carry a little tape recorder around with you. When you want to make an entry on tape, press the "record" button, say the date into the microphone, and start talking. You can even create your own sound effects. (Did you know that water running in the sink can sound like a babbling brook?)

A journal on videotape is a little more complicated (and expensive). If you don't have a video camera at home, you might be able to borrow one from a library or rent one from a video store to record a special occasion. A music or dance recital, a school play, or an important game can become a part of your journal.

Journal Supplies

Here are a few supplies you can use to make your journal more exciting.

Scissors. Cut out pictures from magazines, catalogs, greeting cards, wrapping paper, or anything else and glue them to the pages of your journal.

Glue. Glue sticks or rubber cement work well because they aren't as messy as liquid glue. (But any kind of glue will do.)

Glitter. I wouldn't suggest using glitter too often, because no matter how careful you are, glitter seems to get all over the place. But go ahead and use glitter to add some sparkle for a special occasion.

Stickers. Stickers are cute and fun to collect! Stick them anywhere in your journal or on the cover.

Paint. Watercolor or acrylic paints work well in a journal. If you have a painting set, be creative on the pages of your journal.

Markers. Draw and doodle all over the place—even write entries with marker.

Crayons. Use crayons to decorate the pages or the cover of your journal. It might be fun to make your own coloring book journal by drawing outlines with a pen or pencil, then coloring them in with crayons.

Tape. You might want to tape things in your journal or fix ripped pages.

Photo corners. These hold photos in your journal.

Now you have the basics, but feel free to use whatever else you want.

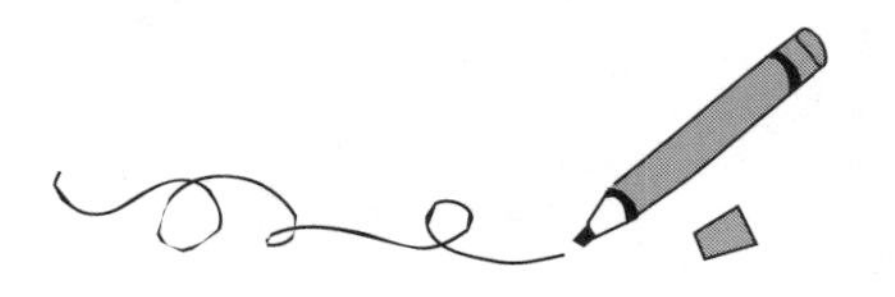

Mind your own beeeeeswax!
PRIVATE!

⋆ For Your Eyes Only ⋆

Sometimes, people may want to look in your journal. They may think you are writing things about them (maybe you are!), or they may just want some juicy gossip. It might be enough to tell your family and friends, "My journal is private, so please don't read it." It's probably safer if some people (like your brothers and sisters) don't know you have a journal. Either way, don't leave your journal lying around. Why tempt someone to open it?

For more ideas about keeping your journal private and personal, read on.

Your Journal Is Private!

If you worry too much about people reading your journal, you won't be able to be honest with yourself. Remember, your journal is the absolutely true book about *you!* Only when you're sure that your journal is FOR YOUR EYES ONLY will you be able to write truthfully about your secrets, wishes, and dreams.

Your journal is your private place to spill out your feelings. If someone (like your mom or dad or a friend) reads something you wrote, that person might take it the wrong way, feel hurt or mad, or worry about you. You need to feel free to write what you want. It's better for everybody if your journal is a private, special thing.

(*Tip:* There might be times when you *want* someone else to read your journal. See page 51.)

"Her parents had told her once that they would never read her private notebook. So she had tested them a few times, by leaving it around the house conspicuously, with an almost-invisible hair on it. . . . She had learned that trick from spy novels. But the hair always remained in place. Her parents really hadn't opened it."

from *Anastasia Again* by Lois Lowry

Keep It Locked Up

If your journal doesn't have a lock on it, you may wish to keep it locked up or hidden in a safe place. Do you have a desk drawer where no one looks? Hide it there. If you want to be really safe, buy a lockbox, or find an old trunk or filing cabinet to store your journal in. If you lock up your journal, you can be sure that no one will sneak a peek at it.

Cover It Up

If your journal is a blank book, you can be tricky and put the cover from another book on it. Take the paper jacket off a hardcover book that's about the same size, and place it on your journal. Then stick the journal on the shelf with your other books. No one will ever recognize your journal-in-disguise.

(*Tip:* You don't want other people snooping in your personal things, so remember not to snoop in theirs.)

Naming Your Journal

Some people choose to give their journal a name. Many famous diary keepers have named their journals—Anne Frank did. The diary she kept during World War II was named Kitty. (It's one of the best-loved books of all time.)

You can name your journal after anyone: a friend or relative, a famous person in the present or the past, or a favorite character from a book or movie. You don't have to share the name with anyone else, if you don't want to.

My journals have had many names over the years. One of them was Ali, after my best friend. The one I keep now is Holden, after a character in a book I like.

Of course, you don't have to name your journal. But if you do come up with a name, you might want to write it down right away so you don't forget it.

From My Journal

May 2, 1994

Well, since you are not named Victoria, I think I will have to make you something else.

Here are ideas:

Lily, Anthea, Mariette, Anne, Emily, Felicity, Molly, Addy, or Zoe. Okay. Very well, you are Anne Shirley after one of my favorite book characters, or Anne Frank after her diary. I will see you tomorrow, Anne.

★ Fall Journaling ★

Fall is a time for getting ready for school, going to the pumpkin patch, drinking cider, and making caramel apples. It's also the perfect time for jumping in the leaves (while you're at it, collect some to press in your journal).

Write about some of the signs of fall. What are your favorite ones? Leaves changing color? Geese and ducks flying overhead? Write down the best and worst things about fall. In this chapter, you'll find fun ideas for things to do in your journal during autumn.

From My Journal

September 15, 1996

Today is fall. It looks like fall, smells like fall, feels like fall. It has that smell of leaves, and the wind feels like apples (don't ask). I can hear people working outside. It is kind of a bittersweet time. I think of falls past—here, other places . . . it makes me want to cry and laugh at the same time.

And I am listening to the Indigo Girls right now. Oh, this is a strange feeling.

Back-to-School Journal

The first day of school is an exciting time every year. Maybe you look forward to it, or maybe you're a little scared . . . but I know you have some feelings about it. For this reason, you may want to make a journal about school.

You could start this journal a few days before school begins. Did you get any cool new clothes or supplies for school? Make a list of them. Write down your feelings about the first day of school. Do you feel happy, nervous, or just so-so? Describe what you're feeling and why. You can keep writing in this journal during the school year, and start a new one next year.

Halloween

One of the best parts of Halloween is dressing up. For a few hours, you get to be someone else, like a superhero or movie star. But no matter how you look on the outside, remember that you're *you* under your costume.

What would your dream Halloween costume be like? Describe it in your journal. Then draw a picture of the costume and color it in. Even if you don't wear your dream costume this Halloween, you can still have fun. Get someone to take a picture of you in your actual costume, and glue the photo in your journal.

Ghost Stories

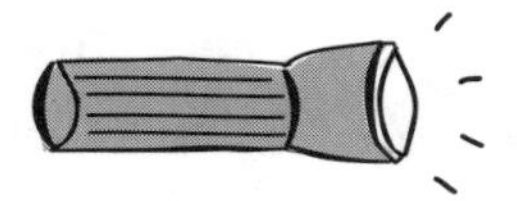

Ah, ghost stories—those scary tales that make the hair on the back of your neck stand up. These stories are even better when told at night, in a dark room, with a flashlight and a bunch of friends. You may have trouble falling asleep later, but the stories are always worth it!

You can write a ghost story of your own. You might read a few ghost stories to get you started, then sit down with a pen or pencil and your journal. First, write some ideas about what kind of story you want. Is your story going to take place in the past, the present, or the future? Will it involve a creaky old house? A scary monster? A noise under the bed . . . ?

Now you're ready to start writing your story. Remember to include descriptions like how the wind sounds or how eerie the moonlight is. This sets the mood for a truly chilling ghost story. Write and rewrite until you've got the story and the ending just the way you want them. The next time your friends ask to hear a ghost story, read them yours. Boo!

Read More About It

Need some extra help? You might want to look at these books for ideas:

In a Creepy, Creepy Place by Judith Gorog (New York: HarperTrophy, 1998). These great stories are funny as well as scary.

Short and Shivery by Robert D. San Souci (New York: Doubleday, 1989). This book is a collection of spooky stories from around the world.

Thanksgiving

For thousands of years, people all over the world have celebrated the harvest with a feast. Today, Thanksgiving is a holiday when we get together with our families and give thanks for what we have.

Write about this in your journal. What are you thankful for and why? You might appreciate big things like family and friends or little things like your new sneakers. Also on this day, think of the people who may not have as much to be grateful for. Be extra thankful that you are so fortunate.

Here are a few things I'm thankful for:

my journal

my family 

food

traveling

Ali and Lindsey and Amanda

my dog, Wuggie 

my teachers

Anne of Green Gables stories

my bike

Fall Calendar

Here are a few ideas for fall holidays you can celebrate in your journal.

September 5—Be Late for Something Day

Relax. Take it easy. Lie back and watch the clouds drift by. Write about how it feels to be lazy today.

October 16—Dictionary Day

Look up the meaning of a word you never heard before or one you're curious to learn about. Record it in your journal. Practice saying the word. Can you think of some ways to use it in a conversation? Here are some examples to get you started:

onomatopoeia googol
incongruous ubiquitous

October 17—Black Poetry Day

Nikki Giovanni, Langston Hughes, and Eloise Greenfield are a few of the poets whose verse you could read today. After reading a few poems, you might be inspired to write your own in your journal.

November 29—Celebrate Louisa May Alcott

Author Louisa May Alcott was born on this day in 1832. One of her best-loved books is *Little Women*. My favorite character in the book is Jo March, a tomboy who wants to be a writer. If you don't know the story, get the book and start reading. Or you can rent the movie—there are several versions.

> "I'd have rooms piled high with books, and I'd write out of a magic inkstand. . . . I want to do something . . . heroic or wonderful that won't be forgotten."
>
> Jo March in *Little Women* by Louisa May Alcott

★ Friends, Family, and Fun ★

While most of your journal is about you, some of your entries might mention the people who are special to you—like your friends and family members. Sometimes you love them, and sometimes they drive you absolutely nuts! Either way, they can be fun to write about.

This section gives you lots of ways to write about the important people in your life. You can even do some of these activities together, if you'd like.

Friends

Most of the time you can't choose the people in your family, but you can choose who your friends are. In fact, you can make a new friend any time you want—like today.

What are some good ways to make a friend? List some ideas in your journal. Then try one of them. Use your journal to write about what happens.

Fun Friendship Fill-In

There are lots of ways to write about your friends in your journal. Here are some ideas to get you started:

- My friends are . . .

  (List their names, nicknames, ages, likes, dislikes, and so on. If you want, include photos or drawings.)

- The qualities of a best friend are . . .

  (What do you look for in a friend? What makes a best friend better than the rest?)

- For fun, we like to . . .

  (What do you and your friends do for fun? Write stories? Ride bikes? Play sports?)

- If we could, we would . . .

  (There must be something you'd like to try, but haven't yet.)

A Friendship Journal

You can keep a friendship journal on videotape, on cassette tape, or in a notebook. A friendship journal is great for keeping in touch with friends who live far away. Here's how it works: You keep it for a while, writing or recording whatever you want. Then you give it to your friend (or send it, if your friend lives far away). Your friend does the same and sends it back, and so on.

Speaking of friends, sometimes a friend may ask to see your personal journal. Maybe you don't want to share. What should you do?

It's okay to keep your personal journal private, even if your best friend asks you to share it. If you aren't sure what to do, take some time to think about it. In the book *Amelia Writes Again,* Amelia faces this problem when her best friend asks to see the special notebook that holds Amelia's private thoughts.

> "I just don't know if I should show her. It's hard to decide. Some things should just be for yourself, but some things are okay to share with your best friend."
>
> from *Amelia Writes Again* by Marissa Moss

Read the book to find out what Amelia did next. (*Hint:* It has something to do with what these two pages are about!)

Fights with Friends

Friends can be one of the best things in the world, but they can also cause some problems. Your journal can help you solve a problem with a friend before it turns into a major fight.

Write about the problem in your journal. On a blank page, you might write all the mean things you'd like to tell your friend, just to blow off steam. (This is much better than saying these things to her face.) When you're finished writing, rip the page out of your journal, tear it up, and throw the pieces in the trash. Imagine that you're throwing away your bad feelings as well.

When you think you're ready, call your friend and let her know how you feel. Listen to her side of the story. Try to work things out and start being friends again.

Your Family

Your family is more than a group of people who live in the same place. You are probably related to each other and spend a lot of time together. You may share some of the same ideas and opinions and know things about each other that no one else knows. If your family drives you crazy now and then, that's normal. Your journal can help you find ways to have more fun with your family and handle your everyday problems, too.

Your Family Tree

A family tree is way to chart information about your parents, grandparents, and great-grandparents. Some family trees go back even further. Family trees can include these facts about each person:

- full name
- date and place of birth
- date and place of marriage
- date and place of death

Finding the details for your living relatives is easy—just ask them! As you go further back, you may have to do some detective work. Talk to older relatives and look through family scrapbooks. Visit the genealogy section (*genealogy* is the study of family history) at your local library. Be creative! Collect photos and other personal items that belonged to your family members. If you discover interesting facts about your family, write them in your journal.

Your family tree may be a simple chart on a single page of your journal, or you might draw a colorful picture of a tree and write some or all of the information on the branches. You can share your family tree with your parents, brothers and sisters, and other relatives, if you'd like. You may even want to show it to your own children someday.

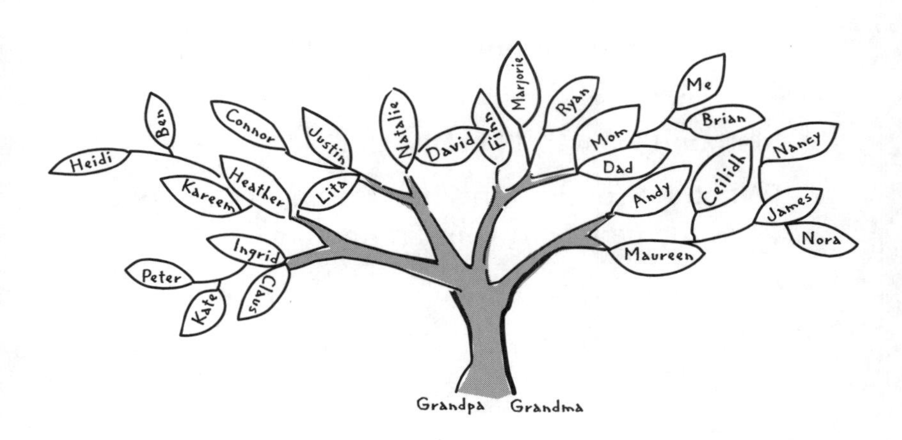

Fun Family Fill-In

In your journal, complete these sentences:

- The people in my family are . . .

  (This includes your immediate family—dad, mom, sisters, and brothers—and your extended family—aunts, uncles, cousins, and grandparents.)

- My family has fun when . . .

  (What are some fun things your family does together?)

- My family is weird because . . .

  (What are some funny habits or odd personality traits the people in your family have?)

- Our family rules are . . .

  (What are the rules in your home? Who does what chores?)

Not-So-Good Times

Much of the time, things probably go along just fine with you and your family. But sometimes bad things happen. You might fight, your parents might get divorced, or you might have to deal with the loss of a special person in your life. Your journal can help you get through these difficult times.

If you're mad or sad or confused, write about your feelings in your journal. Draw pictures that show how you feel. You might want to share your words and drawings with someone you trust. This can help you feel better.

Sometimes your problems feel *too* big to handle on your own. If this happens, talk to an adult who will understand.

Moving

Your journal can be a great help if you're going through a move. You can write about the things you'll miss and how you feel about moving. Glue photos of your old home in your journal. You might even start a friendship journal (see pages 44–45) with a friend you're leaving behind.

Also write about the new place you're going to. Describe what you like and don't like about your new home and neighborhood. As you make new friends, take photos of them and collect the photos in your journal. What are your friends' names? Why are they your friends?

You'll probably still miss the place you left, but before you know it, this new place should start to feel like home.

From My Journal

August 8, 1992

I recently moved from Pennsylvania to Wisconsin. I am in Wisconsin now. But I miss my best friend Ali soooo much! For old times' sake I am listening to New Kids on the Block music and holding my Cabbage Patch Kids. I called Ali but she wasn't home, so I left a message. I hope she calls back. Thanks for listening. It made me feel better. I am so sad 'cause I miss her.

Pets

Pets can be an important part of a person's life. If you have a dog or a cat or a fish or a hamster, you probably know what I mean.

You can set aside a section of your journal to tell about your pet. Write about the funny things it does, and why it is so special to you. Add photos of your pet if you like, or draw pictures of it.

If your pet is a puppy or a kitten or another young animal, start a "baby book" for it. Write about how big it's getting, or if it switches to a new kind of food. Your baby book can help you celebrate your special pet and all the fun times you have.

From My Journal

March 13, 1990

Yesterday I got a pug puppy. She's six months old. Her name is Wuggie Norple. I got her name from *The Wuggie Norple Story* by Daniel Pinkwater (one of my favorite books!). That Wuggie Norple is a cat who gets as big as a house. I don't know why, but the name just seems to fit my dog!

Wuggie is very curious. She's very playful and cute. She and my other dog are getting along pretty well, except they eat each other's food.

★ Winter Journaling ★

A lot of exciting things happen in winter—holidays like Hanukkah, Christmas, Ramadan, Kwanzaa, and New Year's Eve. You can use your journal to write about what you do to celebrate.

Winter can also be boring sometimes. It may be cold or rainy, and you're often stuck indoors. When this happens, you can write in your journal while you sit by the fire or watch television.

Winter in My Hometown

I'm used to cold and snowy winters, but winter may be different where you live. In some places, it doesn't get very cold at all, and the only way you know it's winter is by looking at the calendar and the holiday decorations.

Write about some signs of winter where you live. How do you know winter is coming? What do you do to get ready? Do you look for your umbrella or winter jacket? Dig out your skates? What are the best parts of winter where you are? What are the worst?

From My Journal

February 25, 1993

Yesterday was a snow day, but today's not. I don't know why, because it's still snowing. Outside, the snow is coming down in big, soft, luscious flakes. How beautiful.

Wish Lists

Many people exchange gifts during the winter holidays. Now might be a good time to make a list of the presents you'd like to get. You might want a small thing, like a bottle of purple nail polish. Or you might want something huge and amazing, like a trip to the moon. You may not get everything you ask for, of course, but it's fun to write it down anyway.

Also write about your secret wish for our planet. Do you wish for world peace? Kindness to animals? Presents for everyone on earth?

In your journal, write down some things you might do to help your secret wish come true. Make a list of your top ten ideas. Is there one you can try today?

The True Meaning of the Holidays

Christmas is my favorite winter holiday. I'm ready for the big day as soon as we put up the tree. I just love buying gifts and eating Christmas cookies!

I know, though, that the winter holidays mean more than presents and cookies. They are about love and kindness and doing good things for other people—not just getting good things for myself.

Do you celebrate Christmas, Hanukkah, Kwanzaa, Ramadan, or another special time? In your journal, write about what your favorite winter holiday means to you. You might write about a religious meaning or the caring and friendly spirit of the season. Make a list of some things you can do to share the meaning of the holidays with other people. (Maybe you and an adult could bake cookies for a neighbor. Or you could make a card for someone who's in the hospital.) Give one of your ideas a try.

Making Holiday Paper

Winter has many colors: white snow, green pine trees, blue and red and yellow lights. You can make colorful holiday paper to celebrate the season.

Start with a plain sheet of paper or poster board, any color. You might choose white because it makes you think of snow, or you could choose another color that reminds you of your favorite winter holiday. Then decorate your paper however you like. Here are a few ideas:

- Cut snowflakes, ice skates, and winter hats and gloves out of construction paper and use them to make a winter collage.
- If your family gets holiday cards from friends and relatives, cut the cards apart and glue some of your favorite pictures and photos on your paper. (Get permission from your parents first, of course.) Display your artwork so your whole family can enjoy it.

- Draw a picture of a candle holder and candles. Write words around the candles to remind you of the holidays, or write a poem about what the candles mean.

When you're finished, you can write journal entries on your holiday paper, or use it to make your own holiday cards. If you're in the mood, you can even decorate a very large sheet of paper and use it to wrap a present for someone special.

Happy New Year

New Year's Eve or New Year's Day is a good time to write a list of your resolutions in your journal. *Resolutions* are promises you make to improve yourself in the future. These promises can be big or small, and you don't have to share them with anyone else, unless you want to. It's probably best to start with just one or two resolutions. That way, you'll have a better chance of sticking to them. Later, in a few months or at the end of the year, you might want to look back at your resolutions and write about how you did (or didn't) keep your promises.

Chinese New Year

Chinese New Year comes later in the winter. On this holiday, Chinese people all over the world celebrate the customs of their homeland and wish for happiness and good fortune for the coming year. Tell someone "Happy New Year" in Chinese by saying "Gung Hay Fat Choy."

This can be another time to write resolutions or make a list of the interesting things that happened during the last year. In the Chinese zodiac, each year is linked to an animal. For example, 1993 was the Year of the Rooster. Those who are born in the Year of the Rooster are thought to be confident people who believe in their dreams. You may want to find out what the Chinese zodiac says about people who were born in *your* birth year (ask a librarian for help). Do you agree with what the zodiac says about you? Write about it in your journal.

Design a Snow Creature

I just love playing in the snow—sledding, making snow angels, building snow forts and snow-people—and then going inside for a cup of hot chocolate.

In your journal, design a snowman, a snowwoman, or another creature. Describe what it would look like and draw a picture of it. Would you make a dragon? A turtle? A giant with spiky hair? Let your imagination run wild. Design a whole bunch of creatures, if you like.

Next time the snow falls, go outside with some friends or family members, and build something for the whole world to see. Be sure to take a photo for your journal.

What if you don't have any snow? Try something else. You could shape a person out of wet sand, mud, or clay and use twigs and leaves for the arms and legs. Add shells, rocks, and other things from nature as decorations. Do you have a sweet tooth? Use pretzel sticks to connect marshmallows, gumdrops, and jelly beans in the shape of a person. (When you're done, you can eat this creation.) Write about your experiments in your journal, and come up with your own ideas.

Happy Valentine's Day

Valentine's Day (February 14) is a day to think about love. If you're like me, you get a happy feeling inside when you think of the people, places, and things you love. You may not love everything in the same way, but each kind of love is important in its own way.

You probably have a warm place in your heart for your best friend. Why not design a Valentine's Day card for this special person? Glue on pictures cut from magazines, or decorate the card with glitter and stickers. Inside the card, write things you think your friend would like to read. Before giving the card, make a copy of the valentine for yourself (to save in your journal).

To honor your friend, you might create a diamond poem, or *diamonte* (pronounced dye-uh-MON-tay). This is a poem in the shape of a diamond. The next page tells you how to write one.

Line 1: Write the name of a person or thing (the subject of the poem).

Line 2: Write two words that describe your subject.

Line 3: Write three describing words that end in *ing*.

Line 4: Write four more words about your subject.

Line 5: Write three more words that end in *ing*.

Line 6: Write two more describing words.

Line 7: Write a *synonym* (word that means the same) for the subject.

Here's an example:

Ali
sweet, kind
singing, drawing, playing
guitarist, nature-lover, adventurer, giggler
laughing, talking, dancing
happy, smart
friend

Winter Calendar

Winter days can be cold and gray. Why not brighten them up by celebrating these holidays?

December 1—Rosa Parks Day

On this day in 1955, Rosa Parks was riding the bus home after work. She refused to move when a white man asked her to give up her seat. In Alabama (where she lived), the law said that only white people could sit at the front of the bus. Because Rosa Parks was black, she was breaking the law, so she was arrested. Her brave action began the Civil Rights Movement. Do you admire this kind of courage? Write about it in your journal. (You can visit the library to learn more about Rosa Parks.)

January 21—National Hugging Day

This is a day to hug as many people as you can. (Just ask their permission first.) In your journal, make a list of all the people (and animals) you'd like to hug. What makes them huggable?

February—Black History Month

You probably celebrate Black History Month in school. This is a chance to honor African-American people who have done great things in science, medicine, education, writing, sports, music, and other areas. Read about Harriet Tubman, who helped slaves escape. Or George Washington Carver, who invented more than 450 ways to use peanuts and other plants. Or Marian Anderson, who was one of the first African-American opera singers. In your journal, describe what you think is important to learn about during Black History Month.

February 13—Get a Different Name Day

Today is a day to try out any name you like. Look for a Web site or book about baby names to find some interesting girls' names. Try finding a different name for each letter of the alphabet. Write the names and their meanings in your journal. Pick a name for your journal, if you want. If you could have any name, what would you choose? Why?

★ Girl Stuff ★

There are lots of reasons why it's great to be a girl. Here are three of them:

1. Girls are thinking, creative people who care about the world and everyone in it.

2. Girls can choose what they want to do with their lives.

3. Girls help change the world for the better.

This chapter has lots of activities, advice, and fun—just for girls like you. Enjoy!

Adventures

I must admit, I love adventures. Do you? You might like hiking in the woods, flying in airplanes, performing on stage, or reading science fiction novels. In your journal, write about all the kinds of adventures that you love to have or would like to try.

Read More About It

Seven Brave Women by Betsy Hearne (New York: Greenwillow Books, 1997). In this book, you'll find stories of some amazing but not-so-famous women and the many ways they stood up for themselves.

Be a Superhero

You might dream of becoming a superhero, like Wonder Woman or Batgirl. You might imagine having superpowers, rescuing people from evil, and saving the world. In your journal, write about the superpowers you'd like to have. Would you be able to fly? Read minds? See the future?

Remember, though, that you can do important things for other people and the planet without being a superhero. If you team up with a friend, a parent, or a group, you can really make a difference. You might volunteer at an animal shelter or help pick up trash in a park. You might run a race to help raise money to cure a disease. Whatever you do, it will make you and others feel good.

Real Heroes

Women who are real heroes can inspire you to do your best at everything you try. These people can also make you feel great about being a girl. Your heroes might be doctors, lawyers, artists, authors, teachers, moms, or musicians. They could be famous people, characters from books, or members of your family.

In your journal, make a list of your female role models—people you admire and want to be like. One of mine is actress Claire Danes. I also admire Drew Barrymore and Jewel. Take a look at your list. Why are these people special to you? What important things have they done? Whenever you need a little inspiration, read your list of role models to help you get going again.

Get Moving

What kinds of exercise do you like? Maybe you like basketball. Maybe you like softball or gymnastics. Do you take ballet? Do you like to go on nature hikes or ride your bike? Whatever kind of exercise you choose, it will help make you stronger. Write about it in your journal.

You may want to set aside part of your journal to use as an exercise diary. Make a chart where you can write down the date, what kind of exercise you did, and how you felt. Get moving—and, most of all, have fun!

Fashion

Fashion can be a lot of fun. You can wear fancy dresses for special occasions, or put on jeans and a T-shirt to hang out with your friends. How you dress says something about you. In your journal, write about your favorite kinds of fashion. What colors do you like? Do you like to wear hats? If you want, design your dream outfit—an outfit that would be your favorite, if you could have it.

Remember that fashion is a very personal thing. Never wear something just to be cool. Wear what makes you feel comfortable.

"I like to be around women who make me feel good about who I am, and what my body is like, and what I look like, and who I am inside."

Drew Barrymore

Feeling Good

Sometimes you might be feeling tired or a little down. There are many ways to pep yourself up or ease your mind. Here are some ideas to get you started. After you read this list, write some of your own ideas in your journal.

- Turn on some music and dance. In your journal, write a list of your favorite dance songs.
- Paint a mural or a self-portrait. Use your imagination. You might cut clean, unused sponges into pieces and use them to dab paint on your paper.
- Let your feelings out. If you feel angry, go outside and shout or punch your pillow.
- Don't forget: Use your journal to work through your feelings. It's the place to say anything about your most private thoughts and emotions.

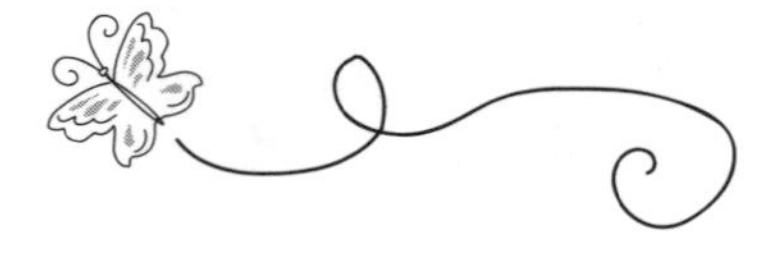

Facing Your Fears

Everybody is afraid of something, and some people are scared of lots of things. Fears are normal. Your journal can help you look at your fears and understand them. It might even help you feel less afraid.

Write about your fears. What are you scared of? Why? What could you do to get over your fear?

Then write down the scariest thing you can imagine happening. Make the story as scary as you can handle, but be sure it ends with you getting over your fear. Once you write and read your story, you might discover that what you thought you were afraid of really isn't so scary after all.

> "Fear is a slinking cat I find beneath the lilacs of my mind."
>
> Sophie Tunnell

Girl Power

Girls can do anything because we have "girl power." I think girl power means you should stand up for yourself and the things that are important to you, no matter what anyone else says. In your journal, write about what girl power means to you. If for some reason you don't feel proud to be a girl, read what you wrote. Maybe it will change your mind.

You can make your own girl power poster or book-cover. Write the words "Girl Power" in your journal or on a large piece of paper. Cut out pictures of smart, strong, and talented girls from magazines and newspapers. Glue all the pictures on your paper. Don't forget to include a drawing or photo of yourself. (You could also start a girl power journal about all the great things you and other girls do.)

Surf the Web

You can get free posters, bookmarks, and bookcovers about girl power from the National Clearinghouse for Alcohol and Drug Information. Visit their Web site at *http://www.health.org/gpower/* or call 1-800-729-6686 for details. (The call is free, too.)

Boys

It can be good to have boys around. You may have some friends who are boys. But sometimes boys can drive you crazy. What can you do to try and understand those sometimes-strange creatures?

You guessed it: You can write about boys in your journal! What boys do you like? Why do you like them? What do they look like? What's the nicest thing a boy has ever said to you? You can also write about the dumb or silly things you've seen boys do. If you want, glue in photos of boys you know, or famous boys you think are cool.

Growing Up

You may be too young to have started puberty yet. Still, you probably know that changes in your body could start by the time you are eight or nine years old. You may be curious, excited, or even a little scared about some of the things that will happen soon. Your journal is a good place to write down some of your questions and worries. You can find answers by talking to an adult you trust (like your mom or an older sister), or by reading a book.

Read More About It

Here's a helpful book about those changes ahead:

Growing Up by Mavis Jukes (New York: Knopf, 1998). This book honestly answers the questions you might be afraid to ask (and a few you may not have thought of).

⋆ Spring Journaling ⋆

Are you ready for spring? The days are warmer and longer, and flowers start to bloom (this is my favorite part!). The trees are filled with singing birds, and you may be filled with all sorts of new ideas for your journal. Write about whatever "springs" to mind.

From My Journal

April 22, 1993

Today is Earth Day!! I am going to write a poem about it and/or spring. I am going home and I am going to play with Amanda. Today is a glorious day.

Oh spring!
Oh spring!
Oh, glorious spring,
How you bring joy and cheer.
And with each wonderful season bring,
The fruits and flowers of yesteryear!

A Nature Journal

Spring is a wonderful time to enjoy nature. In your journal, you can write about all the exciting changes in the earth. Take your journal outside with you and write down what you see, hear, and smell. Write stories about the squirrels, describe the way an April breeze feels, draw pictures of the different animal tracks, or take your journal along on a picnic.

Find small wildflowers growing by the road and press them in your journal. Next to each flower, write a short description of it, and list where and when you found it. Then you can carry springtime with you all year round.

Spring Cleaning

Spring is a great time to get organized. Spring cleaning can help you clear out clutter and get ready for the warmer months to come.

Sort through your journal supplies. Are you running low on anything? Sharpen your colored pencils and put your markers and crayons in order by color. If you have loose journal entries lying around, file them neatly in your journal or in a special folder. That way, your journal and supplies will be ready for you when you need them.

If you like, you can get together with some friends and family members for a big cleaning project. You might clean up a house or a park. Working together can be a fun way to get the job done.

April Fools' Day

In honor of April Fools' Day, make up a "foolish" game to play outside. An easy way to do this is to change the rules of a game you already know. How about playing softball with only two bases? Or playing hockey with a soccer ball? Or you might add a few new rules. Maybe whoever scores a point has to sing a song.

Your game might be completely new. Anything could happen! Players might have to hop on one foot. You might have three teams, or four teams, or no teams at all. Write down the rules in your journal, and give your silly game a name. Then get outside and give that game a try.

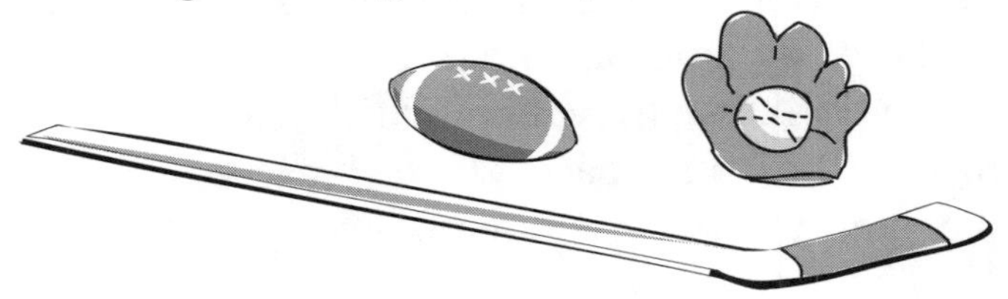

Spring Calendar

There are many reasons to enjoy the spring. Here are some ways to add to the fun.

March—Women's History Month
Now is a good time to learn what women have done to change the world. You could visit the library or use the Internet to find out about important women. You might design a postage stamp to honor a special woman. (Make the design really big so you can add details.) Your stamp could include a picture of what the person looked like and some things that were important to her. Save your stamp in your journal.

March 26—Make Up Your Own Holiday Day
Today is a good day to celebrate anything! Your holiday might honor something that's special to you (like "I Love My Dog Day") or complain about something you don't like (how about "I Hate Cleaning My Room Day"?). Plan a party to celebrate your special holiday. Record your holiday plans in your journal.

April 2—International Children's Book Day

On this day, celebrate children's books and the people who write them. Think about some of your favorite books. What are they about? In your journal, you could write and illustrate your own story for children. If you like, share it with a friend.

May 5—Cinco de Mayo

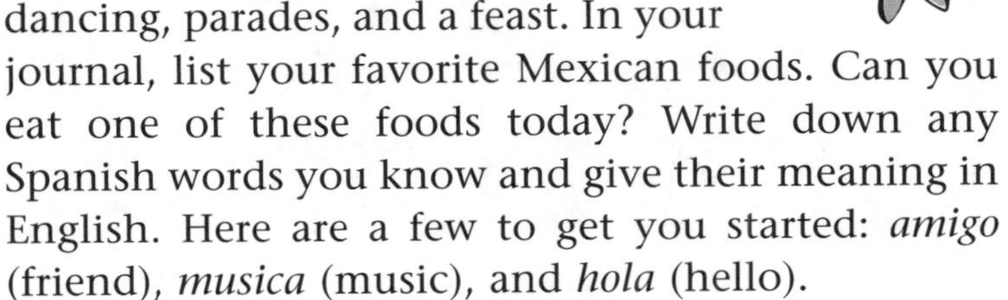

Cinco de Mayo is a national holiday in Mexico. Today, people celebrate Mexican freedom and liberty by having a *fiesta* (party) with singing, dancing, parades, and a feast. In your journal, list your favorite Mexican foods. Can you eat one of these foods today? Write down any Spanish words you know and give their meaning in English. Here are a few to get you started: *amigo* (friend), *musica* (music), and *hola* (hello).

WRITER'S
BLOCK

★ More Ideas ★ for Your Journal

No matter how much you have to write about now, there might be times when you feel out of ideas. This section offers some suggestions to help you through what's known as "writer's block."

Stories with Many Endings

Ending a story more than one way is a lot of fun. Imagine the possibilities! Start with a simple short story. For example, a girl is walking down a hallway, and there are three different doors at the end of the hall. In a regular story, she would probably pick one door. Whatever was behind that door would lead to the end of the story. But in a story with *multiple* (many) endings, you can explore what's behind *every* door. The girl could find a scary monster behind one, an amusement park behind another, and a strange planet behind the last one. Let your imagination run wild, and write a story of your own. When you're done, write the story again, but have the character make some different choices. See what happens. Keep writing new stories until you run out of ideas. The next page has a few story starters to get you going.

★

Gina walked down the street. It was pouring, and she pulled the collar of her jacket higher, trying to protect her face from the cold rain. She didn't notice that . . .

★

Jasmine lay on the floor of her room, looking up at the ceiling fan and the marks that sticky glow-in-the-dark stars had left there. It was July 5th. The summer had barely started, and already it looked like there was no end in sight. She couldn't decide if she should . . .

★

The summer she was eight, Samantha woke up every morning with the sun in her eyes. They were hot days in New York City, days when you could see the steam rising off the pavement, making everything seem like a mirage. One day, Samantha even thought she saw . . .

Cut-Up Poetry

Cut-up poetry is a fun way to write a poem. And it's very simple to do. Just find any magazine, and cut words and letters out of it. Then lay them out on a piece of paper in different ways until you find an arrangement you like. Glue the words and letters down, or rewrite them by hand. There you have it . . . a poem! Create as many cut-up poems as you like.

Here's one of my cut-up poems:

Comics

Do you like reading comics? What ones are your favorites? What do you like best about comics? What do you like least? Try your hand at creating your own comic.

Don't worry about drawing everything perfectly—if you want to draw stick people, that's just fine. You can be the "star" of your comic, or you can make up a character. It's your comic strip, so do whatever you like.

Headlines

Good things and bad things happen in the world every day. Your journal can help you remember the things that are going on around you. Cut headlines and articles out of newspapers and magazines. Include exciting stories or articles about events that sound important. Glue them in your journal, next to the entries you've written yourself. You might add comics or the weather report, too. When you look back through your journal, you'll have a record of worldwide and local events, along with what happened in your own life.

Making Music

Do you have a song inside you? Let it out! First, write the *lyrics* (the words to the song) in your journal. The words can rhyme if you want, but they don't have to. Your lyrics can be about whatever you like—bugs, puppies, summer, dancing, peanut butter sandwiches—it doesn't matter. Nothing is too silly or too serious.

Once you have written the lyrics, write the music that goes with them. If you don't know how to read and write music, that's okay. Simply get a tape recorder with a blank tape, press the "record" button, and sing your words with the melody you've created. If you take music lessons, you might want to create a version of the song for your instrument.

You can sing or play your song to other people or keep it to yourself. It might make you feel good to share your song with someone else. You and a friend could each write and record a song, then sing them together or to each other.

If you write a lot of songs, you can put them together on one tape, or make up different "mixes." If you want, your mix tapes might have special themes (like "music for journaling"). Make as many tapes as you want. In your journal, list the songs on each tape, and tell why each song is special to you. Enjoy mixing and listening to your tapes now. When you're a few years older, listening to them again will be a real blast from the past.

Happy Birthday to You

Birthdays are important days. You're one of a kind, and your birthday is a great time to honor the unique person you are.

In your journal, write about birthdays. What are your birthday plans this year? What was the best birthday you ever had? Why? What do you think are the best things about getting a year older? What are the worst?

Whether it's your birthday or not, make yourself a birthday cake. Have an adult help you make a cake mix from the store or bake a cake from scratch together. Frost the cake, gather your friends and family, light the candles, and make a wish. Then eat your delicious birthday treat!

Stepping Out

Tired of wearing the same old socks? Socks don't have to be dull. In fact, your socks can help you express yourself.

Wouldn't it be cool to have a one-of-a-kind pair of socks designed by *you?* What would those socks look like? Draw a sketch of your own silly or sensational socks. Next, think about what you'll need to make them. List the supplies, gather what you need, and get to work. When your socks are finished, wear them to show off your personal style. Here are a few ideas:

Halloween socks. You'll need orange or black socks, white and orange fabric markers, and black puffy paint. First, draw some ghosts and bats on the socks using the fabric markers. Then outline the drawings with puffy paint. Add your own personal touches to the design. (Make sure your socks are completely dry before you wear them.)

Holiday socks. Start with a pair of colored socks (red, green, black, or yellow), some glitter paint (gold and silver or blue and silver), small bells, and a needle and thread. (Have an adult help you sew or ask permission before doing it by yourself.) First, paint stars, candles, or other symbols on the socks with glitter paint. Then sew bells around the ankles of both socks to let everyone know you're coming to spread holiday cheer!

Beach socks. All you need is a pair of socks (any color), fabric paint or markers, tiny seashells, and a hot glue gun. (ALWAYS have an adult help you with a hot glue gun!) On the socks, paint your favorite summer things—sand castles, slices of watermelon, or whatever you like. Then glue the seashells around the ankles and step out in style this summer.

Future Plans

Planning or dreaming about the future is a good way to learn more about yourself. In your journal, write down things you'd like to do in the days, months, and years to come. Look as many years ahead as you want. If some of the things on your list seem very far away, you could list the steps you'll need to take to make your future dreams happen.

> "Ramona could not understand why grown-ups always talked about how quickly children grew up. Ramona thought growing up was the slowest thing there was."
>
> from *Ramona the Pest* by Beverly Cleary

⋆ Summer Journaling ⋆

Summer is the season of free time, warm weather, and long sunny days. This means you'll have even more time to write in your journal.

Bring your journal with you wherever the summer breezes take you—to camp, to the pool, on vacation, or out in the yard. Get in touch with the world around you and write down your thoughts and feelings as they come to you. I hope you and your journal have a great summer together.

School's Out!

Are you up and out of your seat as soon as the last school bell rings? Many kids are. In your journal, write about school and summer. Make two lists: one of reasons you're glad that school is out, and one of reasons you're sad. Here's an example:

Why I'm Glad School Is Out

- No more homework
- No more tests
- I won't have to ride the bus
- I won't miss things if I'm sick

Why I'm Sad School Is Out

- I won't see all my friends as often
- I might get bored
- I'll miss my favorite teacher

Beach Sand

Believe it or not, you can save beach sand in your journal! Just coat a page (or part of a page) with glue and cover the glue with sand. Wait for the glue to dry. Then hold the paper upright and shake it over a garbage can until the extra sand falls off. Now cover the sand with clear tape so it doesn't fall off and make a mess. Be sure to write down where the beach was and the date you were there. Looking at the page will bring back great memories of sunny days by the water.

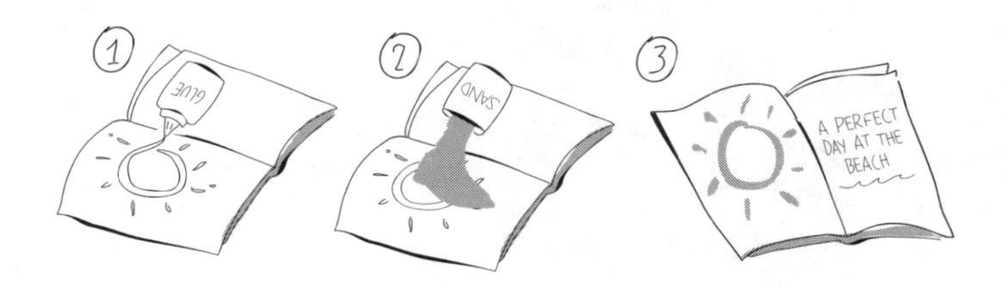

Invent Your Own Milkshake

Does warm summer weather make you crave cold things to eat and drink? This is the perfect time to create a cool treat to share with others. Think of the tastiest milkshake you can imagine. What kind(s) of ice cream would it have in it? Would it have fruit? Would it have toppings, like whipped cream or sprinkles? In your journal, describe the shake, and write a recipe for it. Then ask your dad or mom to help you buy the ingredients and make your dream milkshake. Be sure you make enough to go around!

Here's a recipe based on one of my cousin Kara's favorites:

Banana Split Shake

Put one banana, two scoops of vanilla ice cream or frozen yogurt, and two tablespoons of chocolate syrup into a blender. Blend the mixture until it's smooth. (You can add more or less of the ingredients, if you like. Add a little milk if you want a thinner shake.) Pour the shake into a glass and top it with whipped cream, nuts, and a cherry. Slurp away!

Journal in a Suitcase

For this activity, you'll need:

- plenty of paper
- pens, colored pencils, and markers
- stickers or other decorations
- a glue stick
- a small suitcase or a large shoebox
- a luggage tag

First, sit down in a quiet spot and think of all the places you want to visit someday. Make a list of them. These places could be near or far, in this country or on the other side of the world.

Next, learn more about where you want to go. You could check out books at the library, talk to people you know, search on the Internet, or even get your parents to pick up brochures from a travel agent for you. You might want to find some photos or post-cards of the places, too.

When you have all your information together, make scrapbook pages on pieces of paper. You can use markers or colored pencils, or include stickers and drawings. Glue on postcards and pictures, if you have some.

When your scrapbook pages are finished, put them inside the suitcase or box you chose earlier. Fill the suitcase with other things that remind you of your favorite places. Include a pencil or pen and extra writing paper. (You can use these to write or draw about places you travel to in the future.) Then close the suitcase and put a tag around the handle or on the side. Write your name on one side of the tag, and the date and "My Travel Journal" on the other side.

Your journal in a suitcase is ready to go. Now whenever you go somewhere, you'll have a special place to put your keepsakes, photographs, and journal entries about the trip.

Memory Stones

Many people go on a vacation in the summer. If you do, your journal can help you remember how much fun you had on your trip.

You might collect a stone or seashell from each place you visit. Pick a stone or shell that has a special meaning for you, or one you especially like. It might have pretty colors or be round and smooth.

When you get home, find a fine-point permanent marker. On the back of the stone or shell, write the date and where you were when you found it. If you want to write more, you can make some notes in your journal. Keep all your stones and shells in a special box and store the box in a safe place, so you can enjoy your treasures later.

(*Tip:* You can collect pine cones and leaves in your box, too.)

Start a Book Club

Summer is a good time to read all the books you didn't have time for during the school year. You can do this by yourself, but it's fun to start a book club with some friends. With a book club, you can read different books and talk about why you liked (or didn't like) them. Or you can read the same books and meet to talk about them.

Read the book before your meeting and make some notes about it in your journal. What was your favorite part? Did the characters in the book seem real to you? What would you change? Bring your notes along to help you remember.

At your meeting, you and your friends might dress up like characters in the book and even act out scenes together. Or you can play "Who Am I?" by pretending to be one of the characters and having your friends guess who you are.

Summer Calendar

Here are a few ways to help make the most of those long, sunny afternoons.

June 9—Celebrate Sacagawea

Sacagawea, a Shoshone Indian girl, was 15 years old when the explorers Lewis and Clark hired her as a guide. They traveled together across land that would someday become the western United States. On this day in 1998, the U.S. Mint decided to create a dollar coin with a portrait of Sacagawea. (Banks should have these coins in the year 2000.) You can make a rubbing of this coin, or any coin, by putting a thin sheet of paper over the coin and lightly rubbing the paper with a pencil. Save the paper in your journal.

June 15—Smile Power Day

In your journal, write about why smiling makes you feel good. Draw smiley faces in different shapes, sizes, and colors. When you're out and about, smile at the people you see. Maybe they'll smile back.

July 24—Celebrate Amelia Earhart

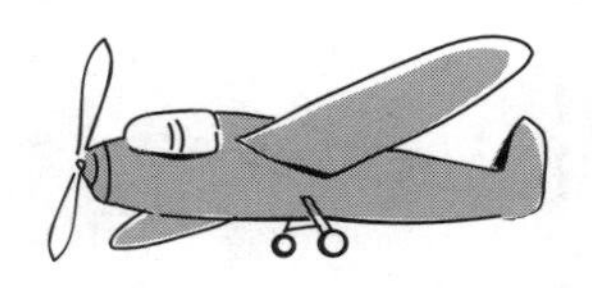

Amelia Earhart loved to fly. In 1937, she and a copilot tried to be the first people to fly around the world. With a few thousand miles to go, they disappeared without a trace. Many people have come up with their own ideas about what happened to the two flyers and their plane, but no one knows for sure. Today, on Amelia Earhart's birthday, write a story in your journal about what you think happened to her. Can you make your own ending to her story?

August 28—Dream Day

If you remember any of your nighttime dreams, write about them. Tell and illustrate the story of what happened in each dream. Write about daydreams, too. Did all of your dreams for the summer come true?

From My Journal

April 20, 1993

My brain is constantly aswirl with silly thoughts. You know, it seems to me that keeping a journal has made me older and wiser. Now, since I have my two journals, it seems that when I am a year older instead of just upping a number, I can truly say I FEEL older.

A Final Word

Dear Reader,

I hope you enjoyed this book. Now you know that keeping a journal is a fun way to be creative and learn about yourself. I hope you will want to keep journaling for a long time to come.

Everything you write and everything you think is important. Your journal is a safe place to explore your feelings and dreams. Once you start journaling, you may not want to stop. I know *I* never will.

Sincerely,

Jessica
Wilber

Find Out More

Books

Amelia's Notebook (Berkeley, CA: Tricycle Press, 1995) and *Amelia Writes Again* (Berkeley, CA: Tricycle Press, 1996), both by Marissa Moss. Read these books (and others by the same author) and sneak a peek at Amelia's journals.

Anastasia Krupnik (New York: Dell Publishing Company, 1998) and *Anastasia Again* (New York: Dell Yearling Books, 1982), both by Lois Lowry. In these books, you'll meet Anastasia, who keeps track of the major events in her life in her green notebook.

Best Friends: Tons of Crazy, Cool Things to Do with Your Girlfriends by Lisa Albregts and Elizabeth Cape (Chicago: Chicago Review Press, 1998). Written by two best friends, this book has all sorts of ways for girls to have fun together.

Clever Letters: Fun Ways to Wiggle Your Words by Laura Allen (Middleton, WI: Pleasant Company, 1997). In this book, you'll find super ideas for making stationery and notes, creating fun lettering styles, and more.

Magazines

New Moon: The Magazine for Girls and Their Dreams
P.O. Box 3587
Duluth, MN 55803-3587
http://www.newmoon.org
1-800-381-4743

Girls and adults work together on this magazine that gives girls a chance to explore their dreams and ideas.

Stone Soup
P.O. Box 83
Santa Cruz, CA 95063
http://www.stonesoup.com
1-800-447-4569

In *Stone Soup,* you'll find true stories, stories that *could* be true, poems, artwork, book reviews, activities, and other fun things by and for kids.

Web Sites

The Diary Project

http://www.diaryproject.com

The Diary Project is a site where young people can share their secrets and feelings. You can read the diary entries that others have posted on the site, or you can post your own entries. You don't even have to give your name!

A Girl's World Online Clubhouse

http://www.agirlsworld.com

This Web site is the space where "girls rule the web!" You'll find strange-but-true facts, career adventures, chat rooms, entertainment news, sports stories, games, projects, books, and more.

Planet Girl

http://www.planetgirl.com

Planet Girl is an online meeting place for girls to chat, exchange messages, play games, and discover technology. The site is also home to a weekly serial featuring cool characters who are, of course, girls.

Index

About the Author

Jessica Wilber is 17 years old and lives in Racine, Wisconsin, with her parents and pug dog named Wuggie. She is homeschooled, and has been for all of high school. She used to have a monthly column on the Teen Page of her local newspaper. Her first book, *Totally Private & Personal: Journaling Ideas for Girls and Young Women,* was published when she was 14 years old.

Jessica loves to travel, read, write, sing, play guitar and piano, create films, and surf the Internet. Some of her favorite places to visit are Washington, D.C., and Chicago, Illinois. After high school, she would like to go into screenwriting or music journalism.

Other Great Books from Free Spirit

Totally Private & Personal

Journaling Ideas for Girls and Young Women

by Jessica Wilber

Written by a fourteen-year-old, this book offers personal insights, experiences, and guidance—journaling tips and suggestions, advice about being a girl, things to do, and more. Serious and funny, upbeat and down-to-earth. For ages 11–16.

$8.95; 168 pp.; softcover; 5⅛" x 7⅜"

I Like Being Me

Poems for Children About Feeling Special, Appreciating Others, and Getting Along

by Judy Lalli, photographs by Douglas L. Mason-Fry

Rhyming poems and black and white photographs explore issues important to young children—being kind, solving problems, and more. For ages 3–8.

$8.95; 64 pp.; softcover; B&W photos; 8¼" x 7¼"

To place an order or to request a free catalog of Self-Help for Kids® and Self-Help for Teens® materials, please write, call, email, or visit our Web site:

Free Spirit Publishing Inc.
400 First Avenue North • Suite 616 • Minneapolis, MN 55401-1724
toll-free 800.735.7323 • local 612.338.2068 • fax 612.337.5050
help4kids@freespirit.com • www.freespirit.com